Indian
Art & Designs
adult color by numbers coloring book

ZenMaster Coloring Books

Copyright © 2016 by ZenMaster
All rights reserved. No part of this publication may be reproduced, distributed, or transmitted in any form or by any means, including photocopying, recording, or other electronic or mechanical methods, without the prior written permission of the publisher.

COLOR TEST PAGE

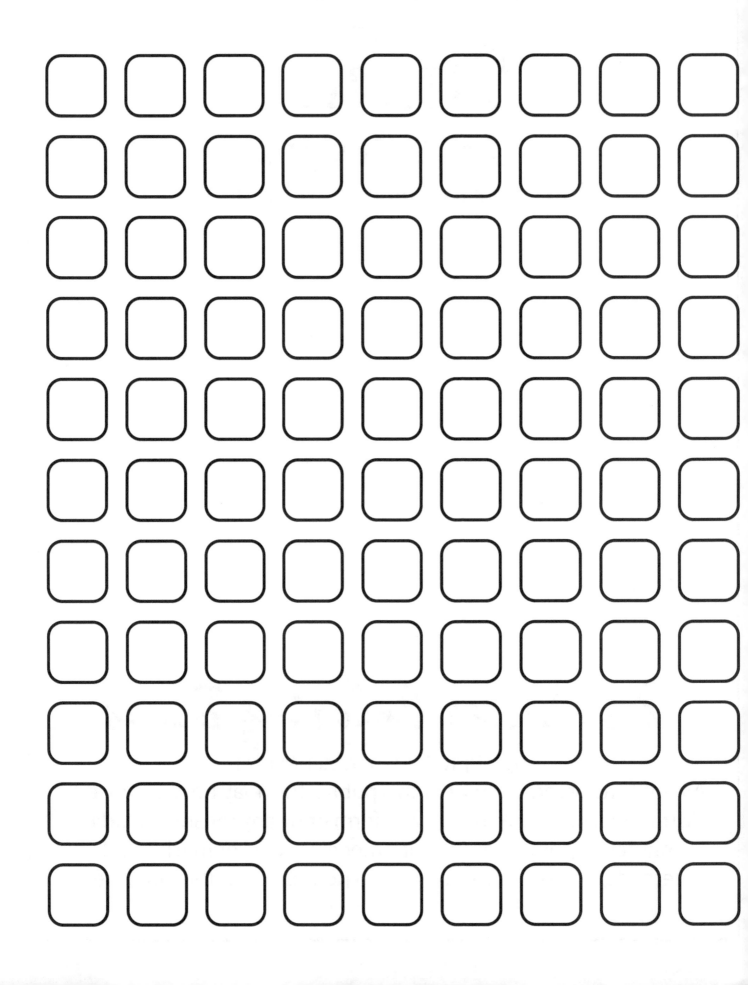

COLOR TEST PAGE

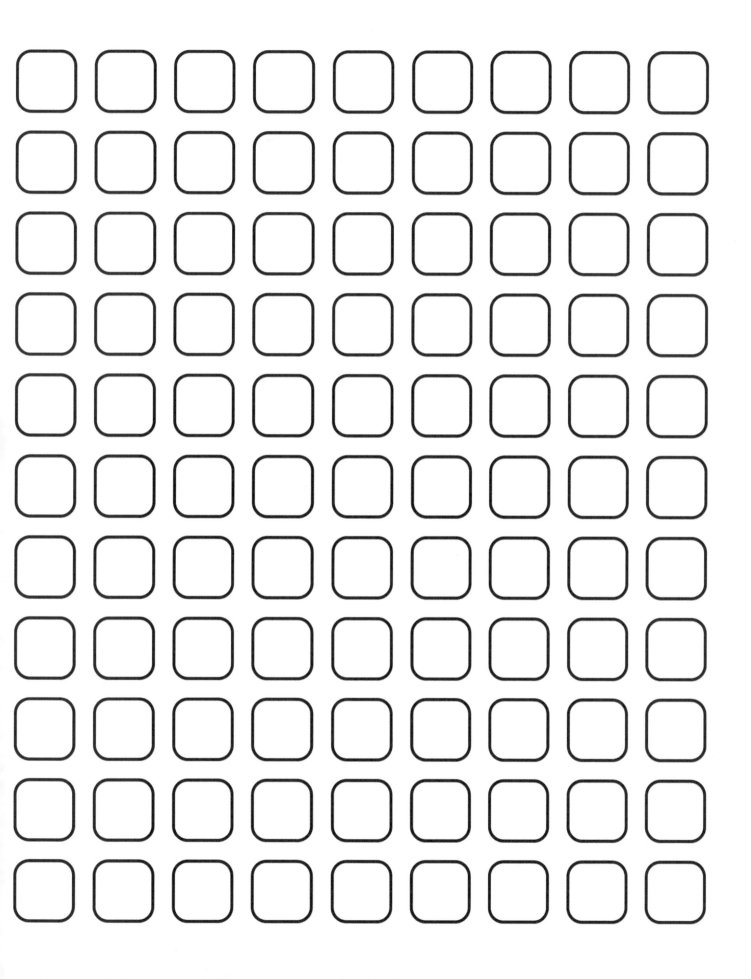

1. Blue
2. Yellow
3. Red
4. Green
5. Dark Brown
6. Violet
7. Black
8. Light Blue
9. Light Yellow
10. Magenta
11. Forest Green
12. Brown
13. Tan
14. Dark Grey
15. Cyan
16. Orange
17. Light Magenta
18. Teal
19. Light Brown
20. Purple
21. Grey
22. Navy
23. Light Orange
24. Dark Red
25. Dark Green
26. Pink
27. Emerald Green

1. Blue
2. Yellow
3. Red
4. Green
5. Dark Brown
6. Violet
7. Black
8. Light Blue
9. Light Yellow
10. Magenta
11. Forest Green
12. Brown
13. Tan
14. Dark Grey
15. Cyan
16. Orange
17. Light Magenta
18. Teal
19. Light Brown
20. Purple
21. Grey
22. Navy
23. Light Orange
24. Dark Red
25. Dark Green
26. Pink
27. Emerald Green

1. Blue
2. Yellow
3. Red
4. Green
5. Dark Brown
6. Violet
7. Black
8. Light Blue
9. Light Yellow
10. Magenta
11. Forest Green
12. Brown
13. Tan
14. Dark Grey
15. Cyan
16. Orange
17. Light Magenta
18. Teal
19. Light Brown
20. Purple
21. Grey
22. Navy
23. Light Orange
24. Dark Red
25. Dark Green
26. Pink
27. Emerald Green

1. Blue
2. Yellow
3. Red
4. Green
5. Dark Brown
6. Violet
7. Black
8. Light Blue
9. Light Yellow
10. Magenta
11. Forest Green
12. Brown
13. Tan
14. Dark Grey
15. Cyan
16. Orange
17. Light Magenta
18. Teal
19. Light Brown
20. Purple
21. Grey
22. Navy
23. Light Orange
24. Dark Red
25. Dark Green
26. Pink
27. Emerald Green

1. Blue
2. Yellow
3. Red
4. Green
5. Dark Brown
6. Violet
7. Black
8. Light Blue
9. Light Yellow
10. Magenta
11. Forest Green
12. Brown
13. Tan
14. Dark Grey
15. Cyan
16. Orange
17. Light Magenta
18. Teal
19. Light Brown
20. Purple
21. Grey
22. Navy
23. Light Orange
24. Dark Red
25. Dark Green
26. Pink
27. Emerald Green

1. Blue
2. Yellow
3. Red
4. Green
5. Dark Brown
6. Violet
7. Black
8. Light Blue
9. Light Yellow
10. Magenta
11. Forest Green
12. Brown
13. Tan
14. Dark Grey
15. Cyan
16. Orange
17. Light Magenta
18. Teal
19. Light Brown
20. Purple
21. Grey
22. Navy
23. Light Orange
24. Dark Red
25. Dark Green
26. Pink
27. Emerald Green

1. Blue
2. Yellow
3. Red
4. Green
5. Dark Brown
6. Violet
7. Black
8. Light Blue
9. Light Yellow
10. Magenta
11. Forest Green
12. Brown
13. Tan
14. Dark Grey
15. Cyan
16. Orange
17. Light Magenta
18. Teal
19. Light Brown
20. Purple
21. Grey
22. Navy
23. Light Orange
24. Dark Red
25. Dark Green
26. Pink
27. Emerald Green

1. Blue
2. Yellow
3. Red
4. Green
5. Dark Brown
6. Violet
7. Black
8. Light Blue
9. Light Yellow
10. Magenta
11. Forest Green
12. Brown
13. Tan
14. Dark Grey
15. Cyan
16. Orange
17. Light Magenta
18. Teal
19. Light Brown
20. Purple
21. Grey
22. Navy
23. Light Orange
24. Dark Red
25. Dark Green
26. Pink
27. Emerald Green

1. Blue
2. Yellow
3. Red
4. Green
5. Dark Brown
6. Violet
7. Black
8. Light Blue
9. Light Yellow
10. Magenta
11. Forest Green
12. Brown
13. Tan
14. Dark Grey
15. Cyan
16. Orange
17. Light Magenta
18. Teal
19. Light Brown
20. Purple
21. Grey
22. Navy
23. Light Orange
24. Dark Red
25. Dark Green
26. Pink
27. Emerald Green

1. Blue
2. Yellow
3. Red
4. Green
5. Dark Brown
6. Violet
7. Black
8. Light Blue
9. Light Yellow
10. Magenta
11. Forest Green
12. Brown
13. Tan
14. Dark Grey
15. Cyan
16. Orange
17. Light Magenta
18. Teal
19. Light Brown
20. Purple
21. Grey
22. Navy
23. Light Orange
24. Dark Red
25. Dark Green
26. Pink
27. Emerald Green

1. Blue
2. Yellow
3. Red
4. Green
5. Dark Brown
6. Violet
7. Black
8. Light Blue
9. Light Yellow
10. Magenta
11. Forest Green
12. Brown
13. Tan
14. Dark Grey
15. Cyan
16. Orange
17. Light Magenta
18. Teal
19. Light Brown
20. Purple
21. Grey
22. Navy
23. Light Orange
24. Dark Red
25. Dark Green
26. Pink
27. Emerald Green

1. Blue
2. Yellow
3. Red
4. Green
5. Dark Brown
6. Violet
7. Black
8. Light Blue
9. Light Yellow
10. Magenta
11. Forest Green
12. Brown
13. Tan
14. Dark Grey
15. Cyan
16. Orange
17. Light Magenta
18. Teal
19. Light Brown
20. Purple
21. Grey
22. Navy
23. Light Orange
24. Dark Red
25. Dark Green
26. Pink
27. Emerald Green

1. Blue
2. Yellow
3. Red
4. Green
5. Dark Brown
6. Violet
7. Black
8. Light Blue
9. Light Yellow
10. Magenta
11. Forest Green
12. Brown
13. Tan
14. Dark Grey
15. Cyan
16. Orange
17. Light Magenta
18. Teal
19. Light Brown
20. Purple
21. Grey
22. Navy
23. Light Orange
24. Dark Red
25. Dark Green
26. Pink
27. Emerald Green

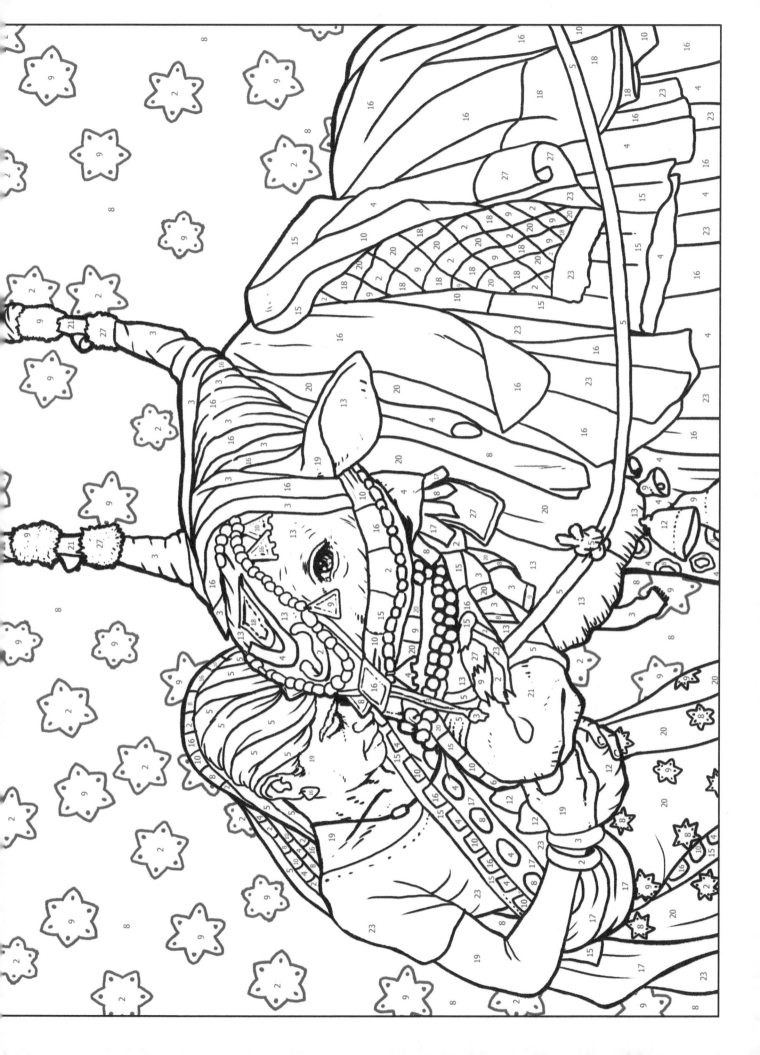

1. Blue
2. Yellow
3. Red
4. Green
5. Dark Brown
6. Violet
7. Black
8. Light Blue
9. Light Yellow
10. Magenta
11. Forest Green
12. Brown
13. Tan
14. Dark Grey
15. Cyan
16. Orange
17. Light Magenta
18. Teal
19. Light Brown
20. Purple
21. Grey
22. Navy
23. Light Orange
24. Dark Red
25. Dark Green
26. Pink
27. Emerald Green

1. Blue
2. Yellow
3. Red
4. Green
5. Dark Brown
6. Violet
7. Black
8. Light Blue
9. Light Yellow
10. Magenta
11. Forest Green
12. Brown
13. Tan
14. Dark Grey
15. Cyan
16. Orange
17. Light Magenta
18. Teal
19. Light Brown
20. Purple
21. Grey
22. Navy
23. Light Orange
24. Dark Red
25. Dark Green
26. Pink
27. Emerald Green

1. Blue
2. Yellow
3. Red
4. Green
5. Dark Brown
6. Violet
7. Black
8. Light Blue
9. Light Yellow
10. Magenta
11. Forest Green
12. Brown
13. Tan
14. Dark Grey
15. Cyan
16. Orange
17. Light Magenta
18. Teal
19. Light Brown
20. Purple
21. Grey
22. Navy
23. Light Orange
24. Dark Red
25. Dark Green
26. Pink
27. Emerald Green

1. Blue
2. Yellow
3. Red
4. Green
5. Dark Brown
6. Violet
7. Black
8. Light Blue
9. Light Yellow
10. Magenta
11. Forest Green
12. Brown
13. Tan
14. Dark Grey
15. Cyan
16. Orange
17. Light Magenta
18. Teal
19. Light Brown
20. Purple
21. Grey
22. Navy
23. Light Orange
24. Dark Red
25. Dark Green
26. Pink
27. Emerald Green

1. Blue
2. Yellow
3. Red
4. Green
5. Dark Brown
6. Violet
7. Black
8. Light Blue
9. Light Yellow
10. Magenta
11. Forest Green
12. Brown
13. Tan
14. Dark Grey
15. Cyan
16. Orange
17. Light Magenta
18. Teal
19. Light Brown
20. Purple
21. Grey
22. Navy
23. Light Orange
24. Dark Red
25. Dark Green
26. Pink
27. Emerald Green

1. Blue
2. Yellow
3. Red
4. Green
5. Dark Brown
6. Violet
7. Black
8. Light Blue
9. Light Yellow
10. Magenta
11. Forest Green
12. Brown
13. Tan
14. Dark Grey
15. Cyan
16. Orange
17. Light Magenta
18. Teal
19. Light Brown
20. Purple
21. Grey
22. Navy
23. Light Orange
24. Dark Red
25. Dark Green
26. Pink
27. Emerald Green

1. Blue
2. Yellow
3. Red
4. Green
5. Dark Brown
6. Violet
7. Black
8. Light Blue
9. Light Yellow
10. Magenta
11. Forest Green
12. Brown
13. Tan
14. Dark Grey
15. Cyan
16. Orange
17. Light Magenta
18. Teal
19. Light Brown
20. Purple
21. Grey
22. Navy
23. Light Orange
24. Dark Red
25. Dark Green
26. Pink
27. Emerald Green

Thank you for supporting
ZenMaster Coloring Books!

I aim to make sure my customers have the most enjoyable and relaxing coloring experience possible and I would love to hear your feedback!

Please leave a review on Amazon and follow me on facebook for updates and free coloring pages!

https://www.facebook.com/zenmastercoloringbooks/

check out more of my books at:
amazon.com/author/zenmastercoloringbooks

Free Bonus Page!
from:

African
Art and Designs coloring book for adults

https://www.amazon.com/dp/1533533431

Also available in color by numbers!!
https://amzn.com/dp/1727708091

And 5x8" Travel Size
https://www.amazon.com/dp/172770830x

Free Bonus Page!
from:

Japanese
Art and Designs Coloring Book for Adults

https://www.amazon.com/dp/153726771x

Also available in color by numbers!!

https://www.amazon.com/dp/1981642242

And 5x8" Travel Size

https://www.amazon.com/dp/1539444066

Free Bonus Page!
from:

Native American
Coloring Book for Adults

https://www.amazon.com/dp/1545034478

Also available in color by numbers!!
https://www.amazon.com/dp/1545034478

Free Bonus Page!
from:

Vogue 1950s
adult coloring book

https://www.amazon.com/dp/1973981521

Also available in color by numbers!!
https://www.amazon.com/dp/1978343884

And 5x8" Travel Size
https://www.amazon.com/dp/1973981610

Free Bonus Page!
from:

Zen Coloring Notebook

https://www.amazon.com/dp/1535457015

Available in 9 different colors!

Also available in 5x8" journal size

https://www.amazon.com/dp/1535540591

Made in United States
Troutdale, OR
04/14/2024